I0815525

The Unexplained

LOST WORLDS

Atlantis, Lemuria, and Mysterious Lands

by Nathan Sommer and Stuart Webb

Minneapolis, Minnesota

Credits

Cover and title page, © Vegorus/Adobe Stock; 4–5, © EnriqueAdobe Stock; 6TL, © araelf/Adobe Stock; 6B, © Peter Hermes Furian/Adobe Stock; 7T, © José Antonio Peñas/Science Source; 7BR, © Iurii Kuzo/Adobe Stock; 8BL, © Public Domain/Wikimedia; 8–9, © Axel/Adobe Stock and © Elenarts/Adobe Stock and © Elenarts/Adobe Stock; 10BL, © sculpies/Adobe Stock; 10BM, © WitRAdobe Stock; 10BR, © Morenovel/Shutterstock; 11T, © mehmet.ozer/Shutterstock; 11BR, © Pius Lee/Adobe Stock; 12, © Dawoudk/Wikimedia; 13, © FAYEZ NURELDINE/Getty Images; 14MR, © Didier Descouens/Wikimedia; 14–15, © IgorZh/Adobe Stock; 15TR, © Zunkir/Wikimedia; 16–17, © Jagoush/Adobe Stock; 17TR, © Rainer Lesniewski/Shutterstock; 17B, © aerial–drone/Adobe Stock; 18L, © Lebrecht Music & Arts/ Alamy Stock Photo; 19TL, © Public Domain/Wikimedia; 19TR, © Public Domain/Wikimedia; 20TL, © Public Domain/Wikimedia; 20B, © Iryna Shpulak/Adobe Stock; 21TR, © Bettmann Archive/Getty Images; 22T, © alina_danilova/Shutterstock; 22MR, © Peter Hermes Furian/Adobe Stock; 23, © Katia Christodoulou/EPA/Shutterstock; 24TL, © Public Domain/Wikimedia; 24–25, © Katya Tsvetkova/Adobe Stock; 26MR, © Edwin Juen Jr./Wikimedia; 28TR, © Chris Willson/Alamy Stock Photo; 29, © Nature Picture Library/Alamy Stock Photo; 31TR, © Sergey Tryapitsyn/Adobe Stock; 31BL, © Peter Hermes Furian/Adobe Stock; 33BR, © Peter Hermes Furian/Adobe Stock; 34TL, © Public Domain/Wikimedia; 36BL, © Peter Hermes Furian/Adobe Stock; 36BR, © Niday Picture Library/Alamy Stock Photo; 37T, © Classic Image/Alamy Stock Photo; 37BL, © Public Domain/Wikimedia; 38B, © Public Domain/Wikimedia; 39TR, © Wirestock/Adobe Stock; 41TR, © Peter Hermes Furian/Adobe Stock; 41B, © lic0001/Adobe Stock; 42BL, © JOHN BAVARO FINE ART/Science Source; 42BR, © Nastya Smirnova RF/Shutterstock; 43T, © Antoine Dorison and Stéphen Rostain/Wikimedia; 43B, © Atelopus/Adobe Stock

Photo Illustrations by Kim Jones.

Bearport Publishing Company Product Development Team

Publisher: Jen Jenson; Director of Product Development: Spencer Brinker; Managing Editor: Allison Juda; Associate Editor: Naomi Reich; Associate Editor: Tiana Tran; Art Director: Colin O'Dea; Designer: Kim Jones; Designer: Kayla Eggert; Product Development Specialist: Owen Hamlin

Statement on Usage of Generative Artificial Intelligence

Bearport Publishing remains committed to publishing high-quality nonfiction books. Therefore, we restrict the use of generative AI to ensure accuracy of all text and visual components pertaining to a book's subject. See BearportPublishing.com for details.

Library of Congress Cataloging-in-Publication Data is available at www.loc.gov or upon request from the publisher.

ISBN: 979-8-89232-887-6 (hardcover)
ISBN: 979-8-89232-917-0 (ebook)

For more information, write to Bearport Publishing, 5357 Penn Avenue South, Minneapolis, MN 55419.

Contents

Lost Worlds

For thousands of years, legends passed down through various cultures have told of mysterious, unknown places and lost civilizations. From Atlantis to Lemuria to El Dorado, stories of hidden realms filled with vast riches have been told around the world. These tales reflect humanity's innate sense of adventure and a desire to explore the unknown. But did these places ever really exist? And if they did, will they ever be found once again?

Water covers about 71 percent of Earth's surface. While humans have explored much of the planet's dry land, the vast majority of the world's oceans remain largely unknown. To date, scientists have mapped only about a quarter of the seafloor, leaving a significant portion of the planet still unexplored.

Atlantis: Plato's Lost City

A statue of Plato

The legendary city of Atlantis was first introduced to the world by the ancient Greek philosopher Plato around 360 BCE. According to Plato, the story was passed down from his grandfather, who originally heard it from an Egyptian priest. Atlantis was said to be located on a large, mountainous, and forested island called Atlas, near the present-day Strait of Gibraltar—the channel between Spain and Morocco connecting the Atlantic Ocean to the Mediterranean Sea.

Believers in the existence of Atlantis claim the city thrived from about 12,000 to 10,000 years ago. Plato described its inhabitants as beings who were half-god and half-human. Many people at the time thought that the world was ruled by ancient Greek gods, with Poseidon, the god of the sea, overseeing Atlantis. The Atlantean civilization was said to be one of the most advanced of its time, serving as the capital of a powerful oceanic empire. Some believe its empire was so vast it may have been larger than the Roman Empire at its peak.

In Plato's writings, Atlantis was to be found at the mouth of the Pillars of Hercules, huge rocky outcroppings located on either side of the Strait of Gibraltar.

According to legend, Atlantis was a stunningly complex city with a unique layout. It was constructed in alternating rings of land and water, connected by bridged canals that allowed for both ships and pedestrians to easily get around. These canals led to a central mountain, where a grand temple dedicated to Poseidon stood, allegedly filled with golden statues. The lush island rings were surrounded by high walls made from shiny minerals, and each had watchtowers with soldiers. The city was also said to be home to a variety of exotic wildlife and to have had abundant natural resources, such as gold and silver.

Poseidon not only was the god of the sea but also ruled over storms, earthquakes, and—surprisingly—horses. Known for his temper, Poseidon was said to cause earthquakes as punishment when he was displeased with those who worshiped him. He was thought to do this by striking his forked staff, known as a trident, against the ground.

In Plato's writings, Atlantis was ruled by 10 kings, all of whom were the children of Poseidon. Each king governed a different part of the empire, and their job was to ensure that their people followed the laws of Poseidon. Plato said these laws were designed to encourage citizens to live humble lives focused on morality rather than wealth or luxury. The philosopher believed that these laws allowed the Atlantean civilization to flourish for thousands of years.

According to Plato, Poseidon's laws also prevented the 10 kings from waging war against one another, instead urging them to rule with wisdom and restraint. As a result, the kings united to protect the empire, forming what was said to be the largest army the world had ever seen. Plato claimed that at its peak, Atlantis had 800,000 foot soldiers, 10,000 chariots, and 1,200 ships. These forces were said to be highly trained, heavily armed, and capable of easily overpowering the armies of other empires.

Plato's accounts of Atlantis are the only writings about the legendary city from that period in ancient Greece. Because of this, some people believe that the philosopher may have invented the story to convey a moral lesson. They suggest that Plato wanted to warn his fellow Greek citizens about the dangers of living a life driven by greed and selfishness.

However, Plato's story of Atlantis ends in tragedy. He said that over time, the people and rulers of Atlantis slowly became corrupt and greedy, abandoning the empire's laws in pursuit of wealth and power. In response, an angry Poseidon unleashed a series of devastating floods, fires, and earthquakes upon the island. According to Plato, these natural disasters caused Atlantis to sink into the sea within a single day, disappearing forever from the surface of Earth.

Lost Atlantean Science

Atlantis is said to have been a utopian society that built huge cities, used advanced farming techniques, and had a thriving economy. Those who believe in Atlantis claim to have found intriguing clues suggesting that the civilization developed technology far ahead of its time—technology that was mostly lost when the island sank into the sea. Some believers argue that evidence of this advanced technology can be found in ancient cultures that may have been part of the Atlantean empire. They suggest that survivors of Atlantis's destruction spread across the world, bringing their knowledge, science, and technology with them.

Supporters of the Atlantis legend often claim that the empire was particularly skilled in architecture. Descriptions of the city mention complex walls layered with precious metals and massive structures featuring spiral staircases and dome-capped towers, which would have been unique for that time. Some believe that evidence of this architectural expertise can be seen in Egypt's pyramids. According to Egyptian records, the pyramids' architect, Thaut, survived a great flood that destroyed his homeland before he settled in Egypt. Believers of Atlantis say that Thaut was from Atlantis and brought with him knowledge that influenced the early Egyptian civilization.

Did survivors of Atlantis move across the globe, bringing with them architectural knowledge that allowed people to build pyramids around the world?

Göbekli Tepe is one of the earliest examples of human construction built for a symbolic purpose.

Others point to the Göbekli Tepe monument in modern-day Turkey, built around 11,000 years ago, as evidence of Atlantean influence. This site features large circular rings arranged with enormous carved stone pillars that stand up to 16 feet (5 m) high. Constructed when metal tools and pottery did not yet exist and when humans were still primarily hunters and gatherers, the monument's complexity baffles historians. Atlantis believers argue that the people in that area lacked the skills and knowledge to create such structures on their own. They claim that settlers from elsewhere—who had mastered the art of building—had shared their expertise. According to believers, this timeline coincides with the period shortly after Atlantis was said to be destroyed.

Some people believe that the Atlanteans played a role in the creation of Egypt's Great Sphinx, a limestone statue with the head of a human and the body of a lion. According to these believers, the Sphinx is much older than traditionally thought and does not resemble other monuments from the same period. They argue that the Egyptians built it using stone-moving techniques originally developed in Atlantis.

Some people also assert that some citizens of Atlantis were skilled miners who extracted valuable metals used in grand construction projects. They claim that Atlanteans developed their mining techniques centuries before others, including finding copper by dropping stones underground and listening for the metal's distinctive ringing sound. In the oral history of the Menominee tribe of Michigan, there are stories of settlers who arrived and dug out what they called the shiny bones of the earth. Some believe this was describing Atlanteans bringing mining expertise to North America after the great flood.

There are those who even suggest that Atlanteans may have created flying machines. The first documented aircraft flight occurred around Plato's time, involving a leather kite large enough to carry a small boy. However, ancient Indian texts describe lightweight, sturdy aircraft called vimanas used in warfare and for long-distance travel. In 1898, a model resembling such an aircraft was found in Egypt's Pa-di-Imen tomb. This wooden artifact, known as the Saqqara Bird, had straight wings and an upright tail fin. Atlantis believers argue that the model is evidence of prehistoric flight technology developed by the Atlanteans.

Fourteen models like the Saqqara Bird have been found in Egypt. Archaeologists believe they date back to some of the earliest periods in Egyptian history. Were the models depictions of ancient technology? Skeptics argue that the Saqqara Bird is merely a model of an ordinary bird rather than an aircraft. They suggest it might have been a child's toy.

Skeptics, on the other hand, reject these controversial theories about Atlantean technology, saying that little to no evidence supports their existence. Some also argue that these claims are insulting to the cultures that have been recognized as the creators of the innovations, such as the ancient Egyptians and Native American peoples. Still, Atlantis believers point out that many examples of lost technology have been rediscovered throughout history. They cite ships allegedly used by the Greeks around Plato's time, which would not be seen again for another 2,000 years. They also mention the cure for scurvy, discovered in 1497 but lost and forgotten for centuries before being widely accepted once more.

Researchers continually find lost technology from the past. This replica of a 3,500-year-old Bronze Age boat took two years to construct and was made without the use of nails or joints. The vessel was successfully launched in 2003, proving the ancient building methods to be surprisingly effective.

What Destroyed Atlantis?

If Atlantis existed, what force could have completely wiped it off the planet? This central point has been explored since Plato first wrote of the mysterious city. Those who believe have many different theories.

The Comet Theory

In 1785, French astronomer G. R. Corli was the first to suggest that Atlantis might have been hit by an object from space. Corli thought a piece of a comet might have broken off and collided with the city, causing it to sink into the ocean. About 100 years later, Atlantis researchers followed up on this, and in 1964, German engineer Otto Muck claimed to have found evidence. Muck discovered two deep-sea holes in the ocean floor along a mountain range he thought was linked to Atlantis. He believed these holes were caused by a small asteroid that broke apart and triggered events that led to the Atlantean empire's destruction.

Astronomer G. R. Corli

Fire from Heaven

In the 1990s, astronomers Victor Clube and Bill Napier proposed that Atlantis could have been destroyed by multiple space impacts. They suggested that Earth had passed through a cloud of debris created when an asteroid or comet broke into many pieces. This idea became known as the Fire from Heaven theory and is sometimes linked to other historical legends. It suggests these tales may be connected and could be based on real events.

Supporters of the comet or asteriod theories also point to an event called the Younger Dryas Impact, which they believe happened around 12,500 years ago, aligning with Plato's description of Atlantis. They argue this event caused fires, floods, and cooler temperatures around the world, leading to the loss of habitats and wildlife. Some say this could explain the fate of Atlantis.

An incomplete animal figurine from Abu Hureyra

Believers claim that more than 30 sites around the world support the Younger Dryas theory. One example is Abu Hureyra, a settlement in Syria. Evidence from this prehistoric archaeological site shows that the area was heated to nearly 4,000 degrees Fahrenheit (2,200°C), suggesting a significant event took place there.

Volcanic Destruction

Another theory about the destruction of Atlantis is that it was destroyed by a volcano. Some suggest that Plato confused the legendary city with the Greek island of Santorini, which had an advanced civilization destroyed around 1500 BCE. Historians think Santorini was hit by a massive earthquake that caused a volcanic eruption. Evidence from the island shows the eruption sent about 10 million tons (9 million t) of gas, rock, and ash into the atmosphere and triggered a tsunami with waves up to 30 ft. (9.1 m) high.

Continental Theories

The Bermuda Triangle is an area near the Bahamas known for the mysterious disappearances of ships and airplanes. Atlantis researcher Charles Berlitz proposed that Atlantis was once a continent near this region. Supporters point to possible underwater human-made structures near the coast of Bimini as evidence for this theory.

Could Atlantis have actually been located somewhere in the mysterious Bermuda Triangle?

Other people believe Atlantis was once in Antarctica. American author Charles Hapgood suggested that the continent may have originally been in a warmer part of Earth. He thought Earth's crust shifted about 12,000 years ago, moving Antarctica to its current icy location. According to Hapgood, the shift may have buried Atlantis under glacial ice, leading to its destruction.

A more direct explanation for the disappearance of Atlantis could be that it sank due to rising waters. As global climates change, sea levels can rise. Scientists estimate that sea levels in the Atlantic Ocean have risen by about 260 ft. (80 m) over the past 12,000 years. This rise has caused many islands to shrink or disappear completely. If Atlantis existed, it could have met the same fate.

In ancient times, the island of Santorini was known as Thera, and the people who lived there were called the Minoans. The Minoans were believed to have been one of Europe's first advanced civilizations. They were among the earliest to use written language and were renowned for their art and architecture. Minoan history has many similarities to the stories of Atlantis. Could they be the same?

The Rediscovery of Atlantis

Plato's account of Atlantis was mostly forgotten for a long time. Even in ancient Greece, people struggled to decide if the story of the lost city was a myth or a real historical event passed down through generations. Some of Plato's students, such as the philosopher Crantor, believed Plato was recounting facts. Others, including Aristotle, humorously suggested that Plato had the ability to create and destroy nations out of thin air. For thousands of years after the fall of the Greek empire, there was very little written about Atlantis.

Interest in Atlantis began to resurface in the 16th and 17th centuries. In 1516, Thomas More's book *Utopia* introduced a fictional island with a peaceful and advanced society similar to the one described in tales of Atlantis. In 1627, English philosopher Francis Bacon's novel *The New Atlantis* used the story of a similar island to explore his vision for the future of technology and humanity. Although these works were fictional, they revived interest in the ideas presented in Plato's ancient story.

An illustration from Thomas More's book depicted the Island of Utopia, his version of a peaceful and advanced society.

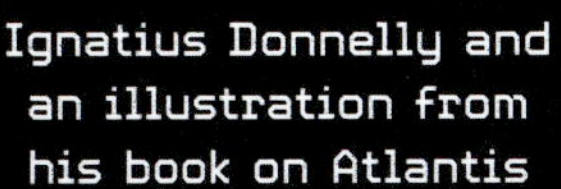

Ignatius Donnelly and an illustration from his book on Atlantis

American politician Ignatius Donnelly played a major role in making Atlantis famous again. His 1882 book, *Atlantis: The Antediluvian World*, was one of the first to argue that Atlantis was an actual place. Donnelly's research popularized the idea that many advanced civilizations stemmed from the knowledge and science of the Atlanteans. His book became a worldwide bestseller and sparked much debate among scientists and historians. Thanks to Donnelly, Plato's once-forgotten story was rediscovered in the modern world.

Donnelly's work attracted many who wanted to continue his research and prove his theories. Rudolf Steiner, for example, was an author and social reformer who claimed that the Atlanteans introduced the concept of good versus evil, which influenced modern legal systems. Charles Berlitz was a teacher known for his language-learning schools. He argued that many languages around the world originated from the one spoken by the Atlanteans. For the first time in thousands of years, people were not only talking about Atlantis but also actively seeking to prove its existence.

Ignatius Donnelly served in the United States House of Representatives from 1863 to 1869. He was known for his unconventional ideas, many of which were unsupported by facts. For example, Donnelly claimed that Francis Bacon, the author of *The New Atlantis*, was actually the true author of William Shakespeare's plays!

The Search for Atlantis

The research vessel RV *Atlantis* was operated by the Woods Hole Oceanographic Institution.

In 1931, oceanographer Henry Bryant Bigelow embarked on the first major expedition to find Atlantis. Bigelow and his crew were aboard a ship named *Atlantis* near Portugal's Azore Islands, studying how strong currents affect weather patterns. They were near the area Plato had described as the location of Atlantis and decided to seize the opportunity to search for the lost city. With only early ocean technology and Plato's story to guide them, Bigelow's team began their underwater investigation.

Other treasure hunters had estimated that evidence of Atlantis might be found about 10 inches (25 cm) beneath the seafloor. Bigelow's plan was to break through the seafloor's thin top layer and use sonar to locate any possible hidden artifacts. He also hoped to collect soil and rock samples to determine if they were once part of dry land. After more than a month of research, Bigelow's team returned without finding any evidence of Atlantis. Some believe that ocean science and technology of the time were not yet advanced enough to uncover the mystery.

According to local folklore, the islands of the Azores were once the tops of the mountains of Atlantis before it sank into the sea.

In 1966, oceanographer James Mavor set out to achieve what Bigelow's crew could not. Mavor was intrigued by the theory that Plato might have confused Atlantis with the Greek island of Santorini. Mavor's early studies of Santorini showed it did indeed closely match Plato's description. This led him to collaborate with Greek scientists to explore the seafloor of the Mediterranean off Santorini's coast. There, they discovered the remains of an ancient city that had existed around 3,500 years earlier.

James Mavor (*center, in white shirt*) directs the excavation of the ruins of the discovered city.

News of the discovery made headlines. The ancient city appeared to have been destroyed by an earthquake and buried under volcanic ash. Mavor estimated that the city covered half a square mile and may have had a population of around 30,000. He noted that the discovery included structures up to three stories tall. Among the ruins, however, there were no human remains, leading some to believe that the inhabitants may have escaped before the destruction. Mavor's findings provided significant evidence for those who believe Atlantis and Santorini are one and the same.

Mavor's team eventually disagreed on who deserved credit for the discovery near Santorini, which led to public and scholarly skepticism about their findings. As a result, many scientists have since avoided researching Atlantis due to the controversy it generates. Some Atlantis enthusiasts believe that this skepticism is one reason why the lost city has yet to be found.

Were the mysterious structures connected to the limestone sinkholes off the coast of Andros Island?

In the 1960s, unusual sightings near Andros Island in the Bahamas intrigued many Atlantis enthusiasts. Andros was the largest but least explored island in the Bahamas due to its swamplands and dense pine forests. It was also the site of mysterious, ring-like structures under the water. In 1992, diver Dino Keller reported spotting a wall-like formation about 3.3 ft. (1 m) beneath the surface while sailing over a shallow coral reef near the island.

In March 2003, Dr. Gregory and Lora Little set out to investigate these sightings. Following Keller's directions, the couple swam about 1,900 ft. (580m) from shore and found the platform Keller had described. The structure measured 1,500 ft. (460 m) long and consisted of large square blocks of stone, with a ramp-like structure leading from the ocean floor to the top. The platform was covered in rectangular holes about 5 in. (13 cm wide and deep.

The Littles believed the platform to be human-made and estimated it could be more than 12,000 years old. They suggested that sea levels were low enough at that time in the past for the structure to have been built on dry land. The Littles speculated that it might have served as a docking station for ships or a breakwater to protect from storms and high tides. Their findings puzzled historians, who thought Andros Island had been uninhabited until the 17th century.

If the structure was indeed human-made, who built it? Many Atlantis believers think the Bahamas is an unlikely location for the lost city, arguing that its islands do not match the mountainous description Plato provided. However, the Littles argue that their findings offer significant evidence of an ancient settlement previously unknown to scientists. Some suggest that the platform might have been built by Atlanteans who relocated to the Bahamas after their homeland was destroyed.

In 2004, American researcher Robert Sarmast announced that he had found evidence of Atlantis near the coast of Cyprus in the Mediterranean. Sarmast claimed he used sonar technology to locate a submerged city with numerous human-made structures. He argued that the city matched Plato's description of Atlantis perfectly and was even arranged around a mountain, just as described in the ancient story.

The Lost Land of Lemuria

Philip Lutley Sclater

In 1864, British zoologist Philip Lutley Sclater made an intriguing observation while studying the animals of Madagascar. He noticed that the island had a much higher number of lemur fossils compared with nearby regions in Africa and India. This led him to believe that Madagascar was the original home of these animals, and he wondered how lemur fossils could be found elsewhere if this were true. He proposed that Madagascar had once been part of a larger landmass connecting India and Africa. He named this supposed continent Lemuria, a lost land he believed had sunk into either the Indian or Pacific Ocean.

Believers describe the Lemurians as simple, spiritual people who were less advanced than the Atlanteans. They are said to have created art, sculptures, and music inspired by their religion but not to have built major cities or large structures in Lemuria like those thought to be in Atlantis.

Sclater's theory of Lemuria quickly gained support from other scientists of the time. In 1870, German biologist Ernst Haeckel suggested that Lemuria might have been the site of the first humans. He proposed that this lost land allowed early humans to travel between Asia and Africa and spread across the globe after the land disappeared. In Indian writings from the 15th century, there were legends of a sunken landmass called Kumari Kandam. Some argued that Kumari Kandam and Lemuria were the same place and might have even existed alongside Atlantis. Historians studying the Pacific Islands noted similar stories in other cultures, leading some to suggest these islands were once part of the same landmass.

Today, Sclater's Lemuria theory is largely rejected by the scientific community. His idea predated the modern study of plate tectonics, which has shown that a continent in the Indian Ocean, such as the one Sclater described, is impossible. While geologists have confirmed that India and Madagascar were once connected, the landmass they were part of broke apart millions of years ago. However, some researchers believe that evidence collected in these areas still hints at the existence of an ancient, previously unknown civilization. Believers argue that there is much more to discover about any Lemurian people and their influence on Asian and African cultures.

Lemurian Evidence

Like Atlantis, the lost land of Lemuria has captured the imaginations of people around the world. Despite scientific reservations, many people still believe and have sought evidence to support the existence of the mysterious continent.

The Banaue Rice Terraces

Some people suggest that the Lemurian people may have been responsible for one of the largest food production systems ever built. The Banaue Rice Terraces, carved into the Philippines's Cordillera Mountain range more than 2,000 years ago, were constructed by the ancestors of the country's Ifugao people. Using only basic hand tools of the time, these ancient Filipinos carved a complex, stair-like rice cultivation system that rises thousands of feet high.

Building and maintaining the Banaue Rice Terraces required immense teamwork from thousands of people over many years. The terraces used canals to bring water from the mountaintop down through the steps, keeping the crops moist throughout the growing season. At its peak, the system is estimated to have produced enough food to feed millions of people. Some claim the original terraces were twice the size they are today. Lemuria believers say this is evidence that a highly advanced, unknown society constructed the terraces.

The Banaue Rice Terraces rise more than 3,000 ft. (920 m) above the valley floor, making them taller than the world's tallest skyscraper. The total length of these terraces is estimated to be about 12,500 miles (20,100 km). If placed end to end, they would stretch halfway around the world!

Wartime Discovery

In 1945, as the U.S. Navy prepared to invade Okinawa Island during World War II (1939–1945), navy divers made a surprising discovery. The navy had provided troops with detailed maps showing the best places to disembark quickly and safely onto the island. However, as several warships neared the coast, they scraped against something underwater that wasn't on the maps. Expecting smooth, open water, the troop commanders feared it might be part of a Japanese surprise attack. They sent a dive team to investigate.

Okinawa is the largest island of the Okinawa Prefecture, the southernmost part of Japan.

The divers plunged into the water. To their amazement, they found what looked like a massive stone platform with wide steps. In their brief report, they described the structure as resembling the remains of an ancient stone building. Could this have been evidence of an unknown society, perhaps like the legendary Lemurians? This was just the beginning of mysterious discoveries in the islands around Okinawa.

The Yonaguni Monument

In 1986, Kihachiro Aratake was diving off the coast of Japan's Ryukyu Islands to observe hammerhead sharks. Instead of sharks, he found a massive, rectangular, pyramid-like structure on the ocean floor. The structure seemed to be made of sandstone blocks arranged in stair-like levels leading to the top. It measured more than 165 ft. (50 m) long and 65 ft. (20 m) wide. Aratake's discovery quickly drew the attention of both sightseers and scientists. Research expeditions in 1986 and 1997 explored the monument, but they could not determine how it got there or how it was made.

Some believers in the lost civilization of Lemuria claim that the Yonaguni Monument is proof of the legendary land's existence. They argue that the structure's sharp angles, straight lines, and stair-like design were clearly made by humans. Researcher Masaaki Kimura notes that the formation also appears to have carvings and statues resembling animals. Kimura also points to holes in the monument, suggesting that posts might have once been attached. Nearby, similar structures exist, leading some to believe that the monument was part of an ancient city.

However, many scientists believe the Yonaguni Monument was shaped by natural underwater processes. They argue that it's not uncommon for sandstone to form straight angles as it erodes. They also suggest that strong currents in the waters around the Ryukyu Islands helped shape the monument. Others think that multiple earthquakes could have split the rocks into different shapes over time. With no conclusive evidence, the debate about the Yonaguni Monument is likely to continue for a long time.

The Jomon people lived in ancient Japan from around 13,000 BCE to 300 BCE. They were hunter-gatherers who, according to historians, made pottery for dishware and carved tools and weapons out of stone. The Jomon were also known for being excellent deep-sea fishers. Still, the question remains—were the Jomon skilled enough to build something as massive as the Yonaguni Monument?

Some believe the Yonaguni Monument was made by the Jomon people.

An illustration of what the spiral staircase may have looked like

The Spiral Staircase

In the spring of 1998, Shun-Ichiroh Moriyama was diving with others when he made a mysterious discovery off the coast of Japan's uninhabited island of Okinoshima. Moriyama saw what appeared to be a row of four massive, round stone towers standing nearly 100 ft. (30 m) tall and about 30 ft. (9 m) wide beneath the surface. He was amazed to see that one of the towers seemed to have a spiral staircase winding around it.

News of the towers quickly made headlines across Japan. Although they were difficult to reach, a wave of divers rushed to Okinoshima to see the structures for themselves. Divers from the University of Fukuoka took on the dangerous task of swimming to the spiral staircase to confirm its existence. They measured the steps to be 4 ft. (1.2 m) wide and up to 15 in. (38 cm) deep. Moriyama's discovery left many wondering how these strange structures ended up in deep water more than 1,300 ft. (400 m) from the mainland—and what their purpose might have been before being submerged.

Mapping the Seafloor

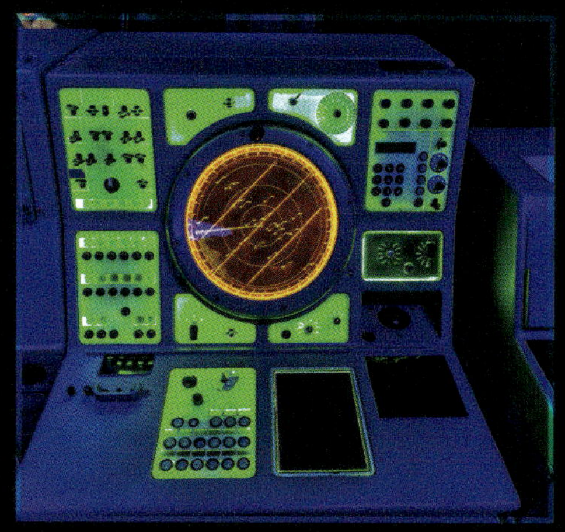

Radar equipment is used for both navigation and exploration.

Over time, many scientists have used sonar technology to map the seafloor of the Pacific Ocean. Their research has revealed no evidence of a mysterious sunken continent. However, these maps do show that many areas beneath the Pacific were once dry land that was likely submerged due to rising sea levels in relatively recent history. This leads many to believe that the mysterious underwater structures found around the Pacific can be explained by natural geological processes.

But Lemuria believers haven't given up hope. Researchers such as Masaaki Kimura argue that it's still possible that a destroyed continent once existed in the area. Much of the Pacific lies within the Ring of Fire, a region known for frequent earthquakes, volcanic activity, and strong typhoons. While one of these natural disasters could have destroyed a rumored lost continent, Lemuria believers still have a long way to go before their ideas are accepted by mainstream history and science.

The Ring of Fire spans approximately 24,900 miles (40,000 km). This area is home to more than 75 percent of the world's volcanoes and is responsible for about 90 percent of the world's earthquakes. The reason for this intense activity is the presence of highly active tectonic plates that overlap and interact beneath Earth's surface.

El Dorado: The Lost City of Gold

As soon as the Spaniards arrived in South America in the 16th century, they began hearing tales of El Dorado. According to legend, a tribe of people with incredible amounts of gold lived in the city of El Dorado, high in the Andes Mountains of what is now Colombia. The tribe was said to be so wealthy that they would celebrate their ruler by covering his entire body in gold dust. The ruler would then dip his gold-covered body into a lake called Guatavita as part of a ceremony to appease a god who was said to live underwater. To complete the ritual, members of the tribe would throw additional gold and jewels into the lake. The story claimed that although this tribe disappeared long before the Spaniards arrived, the lake remained filled with gold.

Having already encountered vast amounts of gold during their short time on the continent, the Spaniards believed the story to be true. Driven by greed for wealth and power, they set out to find the mysterious city of gold. In 1536, explorer Jiménez de Quesada led a team of 900 men on an expedition into the Andes Mountains to find El Dorado. Fewer than 200 men survived. However, in 1537, the explorers did encounter the Muisca people, Colombia's largest Indigenous tribe at the time. De Quesada's team stole vast amounts of gold from the Muiscas, for which he was later punished.

In 1541, Spaniard Gonzalo Pizarro led another expedition into the jungles of the Amazon in search of El Dorado. His team became the first Europeans to explore the world's largest rainforest, but Pizarro's men were cruel, threatening and torturing many Indigenous groups along the way in an attempt to learn El Dorado's location. The local people, however, could not tell them where it was. Pizarro's group lost many men as they struggled in the Andean mountains. The remaining eventually returned starving and empty-handed, having failed to find the city of gold.

Although the multiple missions to find El Dorado failed, the Spaniards did succeed in locating Lake Guatavita in the Andes in 1545. They attempted to drain the lake, which lowered the water level enough to allow them to find hundreds of pieces of gold near the shorelines.

Sir Walter Raleigh

The famed English explorer Sir Walter Raleigh made finding El Dorado a goal. In 1595, he launched an expedition with a team of 250 men along the Orinoco River in what is now Venezuela. Raleigh's crew discovered some gold mines, but they failed to locate the lost city. Upon his return, Raleigh claimed to have found evidence of El Dorado's existence, but many believed he was exaggerating. Soon after, he was imprisoned for 12 years for plotting against the English king, James I.

After his release in 1617, Raleigh almost immediately began a second search for the lost city of gold. This time, he brought a team of 400 men with him. Raleigh was now much older and weaker, so his son Watt led the expedition. The mission ended in disaster, as Raleigh's crew repeatedly clashed with Spanish troops. Raleigh's son and four crew members were killed in a deadly battle, and evidence of El Dorado continued to evade them. Upon his return to England, Raleigh was sentenced to death for failing to avoid conflicts with the Spanish, as he had promised to do.

After numerous failed expeditions that cost many lives, some began to view El Dorado as a symbol of the greed of European explorers. However, research has shown that there was at least some truth to the tale of the lost city. The Muisca tribe of Colombia did perform a ritual in which they covered their leaders in gold dust. The leaders would then board a raft filled with golden objects and cast themselves into the lake as a sacrifice. Over time, this actual ritual may have evolved into a legend of a city made of gold. Because of this, some still believe that El Dorado might be out there, waiting to be found.

El Dorado means the golden one in Spanish. This name was used to describe the leaders who took part in the rituals performed by the Muisca tribe.

The Seven Cities of Gold

While the Spaniards searched for El Dorado across South America, explorers in North America were on a quest to find the mysterious Seven Cities of Gold. This legend began around 1150 when seven bishops and their followers fled Spain by ship, taking their riches with them. They disappeared without a trace, but stories claim they built seven cities said to be filled with gold on a continent across the Atlantic Ocean.

In 1519, the leader of an Aztec tribe mentioned a place called Chicomoztoc, which the Spanish translated as Place of the Seven Caves. This led to the belief that the legend of the seven cities may be true. The belief was furthered when survivors of a failed Spanish expedition to Florida in 1527 reported meeting members of a tribe who possessed pieces of gold. The members claimed these items came from a distant city rich in gold.

Encouraged by this story, the Spanish sent another expedition in 1539. This one was led by Marcos de Niza. With limited information, de Niza returned after 10 months, claiming to have seen tribes in what is now the state of New Mexico who used dishes made of gold, wore stunning gems, and lived in large homes. He believed these tribes had gotten their wealth from seven large cities he saw from a cliff. However, he claimed the cities were too dangerous to explore with a small group.

Europeans first encountered Zuni territory in 1539 when searching for the Seven Cities of Gold. This photo of Zuni Pueblo was taken around 1900.

A depiction of Francisco Vásquez de Coronado leading an expedition to find the Seven Cities of Gold

n 1540, a much larger group of Spaniards led by Francisco Vásquez de
Coronado also set out to find the Seven Cities of Gold. They ruthlessly
ttacked and stole from many groups of Indigenous peoples but found no
ign of the riches described by de Niza. Realizing that perhaps de Niza had
xaggerated his claims, Coronado's expedition continued north, reaching
vhat is now Kansas. Despite the destruction they caused and the extent of
heir efforts, no evidence of the seven legendary cities was ever found.

The remains of Hawikuh, once the largest Zuni pueblo and a place rumored to be one of the Seven Cities of Gold

Although de Niza had been exaggerating, the large area he saw from the cliff was real. It was known as the Zuni-Cibola Complex. This area was a major center for one of the largest trading networks in North America at the time, enabling goods to travel across much of what is now northern Mexico and the western United States.

The Island of Antillia

Some versions of the story of the Seven Cities say that after escaping their homeland, the seven bishops and their followers settled on an island called Antillia, located to the west of Portugal and Spain. The earliest known account of the island comes from 83 BCE, when the Roman military commander Quintus Sertorius met sailors who claimed to have returned from it. They described Antillia as a paradise with beautiful weather, a peaceful population, and fertile land capable of producing abundant food.

Antillia was mostly ignored until the 15th century, when European explorers began venturing into the Atlantic Ocean. According to the story, the seven bishops founded seven cities on the island and burned their ships to avoid detection. This tale was told so often that Antillia appeared on many maps of the time, often depicted as a perfect rectangle. There were several reported sightings of the island. In 1414, geographer Martin Behaim said a Spanish ship's crew saw it. Portuguese sailors claimed to have docked there during a storm in 1447. Others reported having seen Antillia from the island from Madeira, only for it to have vanished as they approached.

This portolan chart made in 1489 is an example of a medieval sea chart. These nautical maps were drawn by hand and focused almost entirely on the coastal regions of the Mediterranean Sea.

Some believe the rectangular shape shown on maps for Antillia might have been mistaken for Puerto Rico. The similarities between the two islands contributed to the name Antilles being used for the group of islands that includes Puerto Rico.

There are those who claim that Antillia might have been confused with São Miguel, the largest island in the Azores. When discovered in 1427, the Azores were uninhabited, but evidence suggests that earlier Europeans visited. Portuguese explorers found a statue on São Miguel of a man on horseback pointing westward across the sea. Arab geographers had described Antillia as having many volcanoes, something that is true of São Miguel. One of the volcanoes on São Miguel is even named Sete Cidades, meaning seven cities. Could this island be where the mythical seven bishops actually fled?

São Miguel is Portuguese for Saint Michael. The land is also sometimes called The Green Island.

City of the Caesars

The City of the Caesars has been part of the folklore in Chile and Argentina's Patagonia region for hundreds of years. According to the story, the city was located deep in the mountains beside a large blue lake and was said to be inhabited by giants with white skin and blond hair who spoke a strange language. Some believed these giants were Romans who had escaped from ancient Rome after the collapse of their empire. They were said to have brought great treasures of gold and diamonds and to have built a city with stunning silver buildings and stone roads.

Some believe that people of the tribes of South America invented legends like the City of the Caesars to mislead European explorers. They say the local people made up these stories to keep the Europeans occupied with searching for gold, rather than stealing from the tribes as many were known to do.

In 1515, Spanish explorer Juan de Solis claimed to have discovered the City of the Caesars. During an expedition, his team fled into the forest after being attacked by locals in northwestern Argentina. According to de Solis, they stumbled upon a city with people who resembled Europeans. Later, explorer Francisco Cesar also claimed to have found a city made of gold and diamonds in the Andes Mountains. These stories led to an 800-man expedition in 1604 to find the legendary city. The search lasted three months but was eventually abandoned due to disease and starvation. No evidence of the city was ever found.

Patagonia is the region at the southern end of South America, with parts in Chile and Argentina.

Despite the City of the Caesars never having been located, some discoveries have intrigued historians and fueled speculation that the city did once exist. In 1976, a shipwreck off the coast of Rio de Janeiro, Brazil, was found to be carrying Mediterranean cargo from around the year 250 CE. Additionally, bricks from the ancient Mexican city of Comalcalco were engraved with symbols used during the Roman Empire. Pottery from the excavation of an ancient pyramid in Calixtlahuaca, Mexico, depicted European-looking figures with Roman-like hairstyles and caps. Could it be possible that fleeing Romans did reach the Americas after all?

A temple at Calixtlahuaca that was built between 900 and 1520 CE

Modern Discoveries

Scientists and historians are still making new discoveries that some believe could point to the existence of lost cities and ancient civilizations. Some of the most recent findings are intriguing and lead us to ask: How many other lost worlds are waiting to be discovered?

The Denisovans

In 2010, scientists working in Siberia's Altai Mountains found a fingerbone belonging to a previously unknown group of prehistoric humans. These people, called the Denisovans, lived in mountain caves in Asia as far back as 300,000 years ago. Scientists believe the Denisovans had large teeth, wide jaws, and flattened faces. They would have been well-adapted to survive in harsh conditions. In 2024, bones discovered in Tibet showed that the Denisovans lived in caves more than 10,700 ft. (3,300 m) above sea level. While much research is still needed to understand how these ancient humans became extinct, it's exciting to know that some of the oldest human DNA ever found is still being uncovered today!

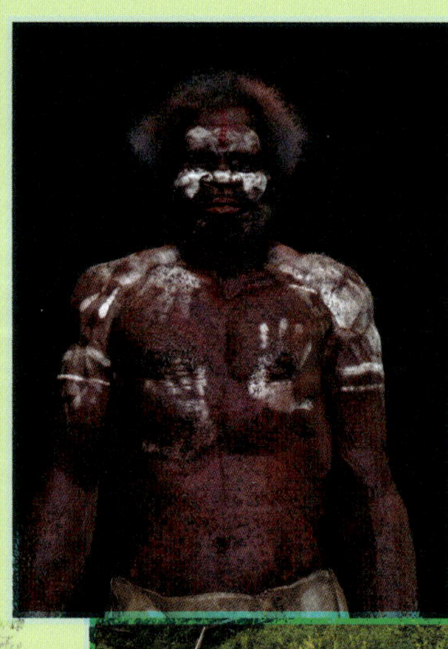

The ancient humans known as Denisovans (*illustration left*) were named after the Denisova Cave (*below*) in Siberia, Russia, where their remains were discovered.

This image of the previously undiscovered ruins in the Amazon was created using Lidar, short for light detection and ranging. This technology uses light pulses sent from airplanes or helicopters to create three-dimensional images of the surface of Earth.

Lost Amazon Cities

In 2024, archaeologists made an astonishing discovery in the rainforests of Ecuador. They found a large network of lost cities buried deep under the dense vegetation. Using laser technology, the researchers found the remains of an ancient civilization estimated to be about 2,500 years old, located in a valley near the Andes mountains. The archaeologists found thousands of mounds and miles of wide, straight roads connecting what appear to be settlements and urban centers. This finding suggests a level of sophistication previously not thought to have existed in the region at that time. Some believe that up to 100,000 people may have once lived in these cities. This discovery challenges earlier beliefs that only small groups of people with simple lifestyles lived in the Amazon thousands of years ago.

The dense vegetation and mountainous terrain of the Amazon rainforests make the area challenging for archaeologists to study. Many experts estimate that only about 10 percent of human history in this region has been uncovered so far.

Glossary

archaeologists people who study human history through remains, artifacts, and the examination of historic sites

architecture the process of designing and constructing buildings

artifact the remains of an object made by humans from the past

asteroid a large, rocky object in space that orbits the sun

astronomer a scientist who studies objects in space

atmosphere the mixture of gases that surrounds Earth

biologist a scientist who studies living things

breakwater a human-made barrier built in a body of water to protect a coast from strong waves

canals human-made waterways that allow boats to travel between bodies of water

cargo goods carried by a vessel or vehicle from one place to another

chariots horse-driven vehicles with two wheels that were used for racing and in battle during ancient times

civilization the way of life in a particular area

comet a large object from space made of ice and dust that orbits the sun

controversial something that creates disagreements between people

coral reef an underwater habitat made up of the skeletons of many small creatures called corals

corrupt to act in an evil or dishonest way

crust the outer layer of Earth

debris what remains of something that is broken down or destroyed

disembarking leaving a ship, aircraft, or other vehicle

economy the system in which goods and services are made and sold

empire a group of states or areas that come together to become one powerful authority

engineer a person who designs and builds machines or processes

evidence objects or information that can be used to prove whether something is true

excavation the digging out of material from the ground

expedition a journey on which a group of people go with a specific goal in mind

extraterrestrial an event or thing from outside of Earth

fertile good for growing plants

fiction stories that describe imaginary events and people

geographer a scientist who studies Earth's surface and land

geologists scientists who study the structure and history of Earth

glacial relating to large masses of snow and ice

investigated worked to find out the facts or the truth about something

legal related to rules and laws

legend a story that is passed down between people over a long period of time

mining the process of removing useful materials from the earth

moats deep, wide human-made ditches that are often filled with water

monument a building, structure, or site with historical importance

morally relating to the motivations that drive a person's behavior and way of life

mysterious causing wonder or curiosity

myth an untrue imagining of a historical event

oceanographer a scientist who studies the ocean

philosopher someone who studies the human mind and the nature of human existence

plate tectonics a scientific theory that explains the constant movement of Earth's crust

prehistoric relating to a time period before written records

ritual a series of actions performed in a cultural or religious ceremony

sacrifice something that is offered or given up to please a god

scurvy a disease caused by a lack of vitamin C in the body

sea level the height of the surface of the sea

settlers people who move from one country to another

skeptics people who are in doubt or disbelief about something

sonar technology that uses sound waves to locate objects underwater

theories ideas used as possible explanations for something

tsunami a giant wave caused by an earthquake or a volcanic eruption under the sea

urban related to a city

utopian states or societies in which things are nearly perfect

vegetation the plants and trees within an area

Read More

Berne, Emma Carlson. *What Do We Know about Atlantis? (What Do We Know About?)*. New York: Penguin Workshop, 2022.

Hansen, Grace. *History's Secrets of the Air and Sea (History's Greatest Mysteries)*. Minneapolis: Pop!, 2023.

Hudak, Heather C. *Lost Kings and Kingdoms (History Raiders)*. New York: Crabtree Publishing Company, 2022.

Mather, Charis. *Earth Myths: Exploded by Science (Totally Not True!)*. Minneapolis: Bearport Publishing Company, 2024.

Learn More Online

1. Go to **FactSurfer.com** or scan the QR code below.
2. Enter "**Lost Worlds**" into the search box.
3. Click on the cover of this book to see a list of websites.

Index